A Note to Parents

Dorling Kindersley Readers is a compelling new program for beginning readers, designed in conjunction with leading literacy experts, including Dr. Linda Gambrell, President of the National Reading Conference and past board member of the International Reading Association.

Beautiful illustrations and superb full-color photographs combine with engaging, easy-to-read stories to offer a fresh approach to each subject in the series. Each *Dorling Kindersley Reader* is guaranteed to capture a child's interest while developing his or her reading skills, general knowledge, and love of reading.

The four levels of *Dorling Kindersley Readers* are aimed at different reading abilities, enabling you to choose the books that are exactly right for your child:

Level 1 – Beginning to read
Level 2 – Beginning to read alone
Level 3 – Reading alone
Level 4 – Proficient readers

The "normal" age at which a child begins to read can be anywhere from three to eight years old, so these levels are intended only as a general guideline.

No matter which level you select, you can be sure that you are helping your child learn to read, then read to learn!

D0092664

1

Dorling **DK** Kindersley

LONDON, NEW YORK, SYDNEY, DELHI, PARIS,
MUNICH and JOHANNESBURG

Project Editor Louise Pritchard
Art Editor Jill Plank
Managing Editor Bridget Gibbs
Senior Art Editor Sarah Ponder
Senior DTP Designer Bridget Roseberry
US Editor Regina Kahney
Production Melanie Dowland
Picture Researchers
Maureen Cowdroy, Frances Vargo
Illustrator Peter Dennis
Jacket Designer Giles Powell-Smith
Indexer Lynn Bresler
Reading Consultant Linda Gambrell, Ph.D.

First American Edition, 2000
2 4 6 8 10 9 7 5 3 1
Published in the United States by DK Publishing, Inc.
95 Madison Avenue, New York, New York 10016

Library of Congress Cataloging-in-Publication Data
Chrisp, Peter.
  Welcome to the Globe!: the story of Shakespeare's theater/by Peter
Chrisp. – 1st American ed.
  p. cm. – (Dorling Kindersley readers)
  Summary: Various characters, including a waterman, an actor, a
gallant, and an appleseller, from Shakespeare's London describe the
Globe Theatre from their own perspective.
  ISBN 0-7894-6641-4 (hardcover) – ISBN 0-7894-6640-6 (pbk.)
  1. Globe Theatre (Southwark, London, England)– Juvenile literature.
2. Shakespeare, William, 1564–1616–Stage history–England–London–
Juvenile literature. 3. Shakespeare, William, 1564–1616–Stage history–
To 1625–Juvenile literature. 4. Theater–England–London–History–17th
century–Juvenile literature. 5. Theaters–England–London–Juvenile
literature. [1. Globe Theatre (Southwark, London, England) 2. London
(England)–Social life and customs–16th century. 3. London (England)–
Social life and customs–17th century.] I. Title. II. Series.

PR2920.C48 2000
792'.09421'6409032–dc21
                                    00-021931

Color reproduction by Colourscan, Singapore
Printed and bound in China by L Rex

The publisher thanks the following for their kind permission
to reproduce their photographs:
c=centre; t=top; b=below; l=left; r=right

Adam Butler/PA Photos, London: 46a; Atkinson Art Gallery,
Southport/Bridgeman Art Library, London: Billie Love Historical
Collection: 26, 36a, 38ar; Dulwich Picture Gallery, London/Bridgeman
Art Library, London: 20a; E.T. Archive, London: 39a; Fitzwilliam
Museum, University of Cambridge, UK/Bridgeman Art Library,
London: 34; Guildhall Library/Bridgeman Art Library, London: 6, 10b;
The Kobal Collection, London: 47a; Mary Evans Picture Library: 8b,
13a, 14, 16a, 17, 25, 37, 38–39b, 44, 45; Philip Mould, Historical
Portraits Ltd, London/Bridgeman Art Library, London: 15; The
Raymond Mander & Joe Mitcheson Theatre Collection Ltd: 20b; Rex
Features: 46a; © Sonia Halliday Photographs: 9b.

see our complete catalogue at
www.dk.com

Contents

WELCOME TO THE GLOBE!

THE STORY OF SHAKESPEARE'S THEATER

Written by Peter Chrisp

A Dorling Kindersley Book

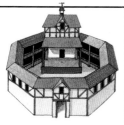

The Globe
"Globe" means "world," and the theater had a motto on the wall. It read: "This whole world is a stage."

A visit to the Globe

It is the summer of 1602 and you are a visitor to London. Why don't you come with us to the Globe playhouse? This famous theater is in Bankside, which is on the south bank of the Thames River.

A cutpurse will tell you how he learned his trade – stealing from people in the audience. See page 34.

Cuthbert Burbage, the company's businessman, will tell you all about his playhouse. See page 8.

A waterman will row you across the Thames River to the Globe. See page 6.

Nick Tooley, a boy player, will tell you what it's like to play the women in Shakespeare's plays. See page 26.

The Globe is one of the sights of London. It has the best actors and the most famous playwright in England – Mr. William Shakespeare.

You will meet all sorts of characters on your visit. They will tell you all you want to know.

Kate Strong, the appleseller, will explain why the Globe has to close down when the plague is raging. See page 38.

A gallant will tell you how he comes to the playhouse to show off his expensive clothes. See page 28.

Richard Burbage, the greatest actor around, will explain to you the tricks of the trade. See page 20.

Bankside
The area called Bankside was the entertainment center of London during the time of Shakespeare.

A groundling, who pays a penny to watch the plays from the yard, will tell you how he enjoys himself at the Globe. See page 30.

The waterman

Are you looking for a boat to cross the river? Let me take you! Otherwise you will have to walk across the bridge. You will not find a man who is better with a pair of oars than me. Look at these arm muscles! They come from 15 years of rowing.

So you're going to see a play at the Globe? I've never been there myself. I'm too busy rowing the playgoers across. My passengers say that it is the best playhouse in London. Richard Burbage is the star there.

See those flags? They are flying over the playhouses. There is a flag flying over the bear garden too, where there is more entertainment.

London Bridge
Playgoers who could not afford the boat fare crossed over the Thames River using London Bridge – the only bridge over the river.

A play today
Flags flew over the playhouses when there was to be a play that day. The playhouses were open to the air. Plays were not put on in bad weather or if rain was likely.

An old print of the Thames in London

The playhouses are taller than all the houses around them. They have to be tall so that everyone can see them. We watermen are always pleased to see the flags flying. We know we'll have a busy day taking the playgoers across.

Here we are already on the south bank of the river. Please take care stepping ashore!

Water taxis
The London watermen were like today's taxi drivers, only on water. They took passengers up, down, and across the Thames River. The river was usually crowded with boats of all sizes.

Business man
Cuthbert Burbage had a long successful career running theaters. He died in 1636 at the age of 70.

Travelers
When traveling players came to town, they put up a stage in the market-place or in the courtyard of an inn. They set up at fairs too.

Theater business

Welcome to the Globe! My name is Cuthbert Burbage and this is my playhouse. I built it with my brother, Richard.

When Richard and I were boys, back in the 1570s, there were no playhouses in England. Our father, James, was a traveling player. His company moved from place to place and put up a temporary stage for their plays. After a show, they passed around a hat to collect pennies from the audience.

In those days, putting on plays was a risky business. The players never knew if they would get a big audience, or if the people would pay up afterwards. Father was a clever man and he knew that he could make a better living. He borrowed some money and in 1576 he built a permanent playhouse just outside London.

Father called the playhouse the Theater, from the Greek word *theatron,* meaning "viewing place." This reminded people that acting is an old and respectable craft.

Greek theater
The ancient Greeks built the first theaters 2,500 years ago. They put on plays as part of religious festivals.

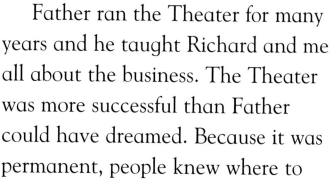

Father ran the Theater for many years and he taught Richard and me all about the business. The Theater was more successful than Father could have dreamed. Because it was permanent, people knew where to go to see a play, and big crowds went to the Theater. The players charged the audience before the show, so they were sure of being paid.

But we had one problem. Father didn't own the land on which the Theater stood. It belonged to a man named Giles Allen. Father had paid him for the right to use his land, but for only 21 years.

The lease, or agreement, ran out in April 1597 and Allen demanded a fortune to renew it. He knew that if Father couldn't pay, he would get to keep the playhouse for himself.

Father argued with Allen about the lease, and he was still arguing when he died, leaving the mess to Richard and me to sort out. I was worrying about it one night when the answer came to me. We would move the playhouse somewhere else!

Reusable wood
Allen wanted to put the wood of the Theater to a "better purpose" than a playhouse.

In December 1598, Richard and I hired some builders. While everyone else was celebrating Christmas, we took apart the Theater, timber by timber. We loaded everything on to a boat and carried it across the river to Bankside, where I'd leased some land cheaply for 31 years.

Timbers
Most English buildings had a frame of oak beams called timbers. They were joined by wooden pegs and could be taken apart.

Using the timbers from the Theater, the builders put up a new playhouse. We called it the Globe. Giles Allen was furious when he found out what we'd done. I wish I'd seen his face when he saw that the playhouse had vanished!

Five player friends helped us to start the company: Will Kemp, Augustine Phillips, Tom Pope, John Hemming, and Will Shakespeare. We seven, called the Sharers, own the Globe. We share all the costs – and the profits.

Good company
As well as the Sharers, the company at the Globe included some musicians, hired players, and odd-job men called stagekeepers.

13

No license
Players who performed without a lord's license could be whipped or branded – marked on the face with a hot iron.

Disapproval
The Puritans disapproved of dancing, music, gambling, and plays. They believed that people should only work and worship God.

By law, all players need a lord or lady to give them permission to perform. A powerful nobleman named the Lord Chamberlain is our protector, and our company is called the Lord Chamberlain's Men.

We need our lord's protection because we have many enemies. We are hated by the Puritans – strict Christians who think that any sort of worldly pleasure is bad. They think that playhouses are wicked. They claim that the crowds who gather to see plays are a threat to law and order.

The city of London is governed by people called aldermen. Most of them are Puritans and they will not let us perform in the city. That is why we built the Globe south of the river, outside the city's boundaries. The aldermen often ask Queen Elizabeth to close the playhouses.

The queen is no Puritan. She loves plays. Her Majesty never comes to the Globe but we perform for her in her palaces at festivals such as Christmas.

Queen Elizabeth I in about 1600

At Court
One of Shakespeare's plays, *The Merry Wives of Windsor*, was especially written to please Queen Elizabeth.

15

Each of our players has his own specialty. My brother Richard always plays the main part because he is the best actor. Tom Pope is an acrobat and Will Kemp is a clown.

Comedies
Comedies such as *Twelfth Night* were light-hearted plays about love, with happy endings. There was often a part for a clown.

Will Shakespeare is a good enough player, but his real talent is writing plays. We put on up to 15 plays a month. Will doesn't have time to write them all so we buy some from other writers too.

We offer something for everyone here at the Globe. Do you like comedies? Will writes plenty of those. Perhaps you prefer the serious stuff. Nobody writes tragedies better than Will. Tragedies are dark plays full of murders and madness.

Will's plays
Shakespeare wrote 38 plays. Most of them were published in a book by his fellow actors after his death in 1616.

We put on history plays, such as *Henry V,* too. These are stories about the kings and queens of England, and the wars that they fought long ago. There's lots of action, with exciting battle scenes and sword fights. The audience loves these, especially when we show English armies beating foreigners.

Tragedies
Tragedies were about the sufferings of great heroes and heroines. They ended with the death of the main character.

Histories
Plays featuring a battle with an English victory were popular in wartime. The country was at war with Spain from 1585 until 1604.

Henry V at the Battle of Agincourt

17

Costly clothes
Each playhouse had expensive costumes for their actors. A velvet cloak embroidered with gold and silver probably cost more than a day's total ticket sales.

Quick change
The tiring house was used as a dressing room. Players often had more than one part in a play, so they had to change into their costumes very quickly.

Would you like to look around the playhouse? The rooms behind the stage are called the tiring house. This is where we keep the costumes. Have you ever seen so many dresses, suits, and wigs? We spend a lot of money on clothes. The audience expects to see the players in dazzling costumes. They would stop coming to the Globe if we wore dull clothes.

I buy many clothes from servants of nobles. The rich give their old clothes to their servants. But it is illegal for servants to wear expensive clothes, so they sell them to us.

Players can wear rich clothes on stage. Richard wears a purple robe trimmed with fur when he is a king. We paid more for this than we paid Will Shakespeare to write the play!

Dress law
Everyone had to wear clothes according to their station, or position in life. People whose clothes were thought to be too expensive were arrested and fined.

Self-portrait
Richard Burbage was a talented painter as well as an actor. This picture may be his self-portrait.

English hero
Henry V was king of England from 1413 to 1422. He invaded France in 1415 and had a great victory over larger French forces.

The star

I am Richard Burbage, the greatest star of all the playhouses. Surely you recognize me! I take on all the leading roles here at the Globe. Kings, heroes, villains, old men, young men, even madmen – I've played them all on this stage.

My brother Cuthbert likes the business side of things.

I love the stage and I feel most alive when I'm standing there, with all the eyes of the audience on me.

Today we're doing an old favorite – *Henry V.* It's all about a great English hero – the king who beat the French at the Battle of Agincourt in 1415. Naturally, I play the famous king.

Will Shakespeare has written lots of rousing speeches for me to deliver. Before the battle, I wave my sword and shout, "On, on, you noblest English!" The crowd roars and cheers. It feels like they would probably follow me into a real battle if they could.

Lifelike
Many players overacted, waving their arms about and shouting. But Richard Burbage was famous for his realistic acting.

21

A scene is set
The players had to set the scene. For example, a lighted candle showed it was nighttime.

In *Henry V* we have to do battle scenes in which we must make the playgoers think they're seeing whole armies going to war. That's not easy with just seven players on a small stage. The trick is to get all the people in the audience to use their imaginations.

Language
Shakespeare's words often put the audience in the picture. The characters might describe night falling, day breaking, or the wind howling.

At the very beginning of the play, we say to the audience, "Let us on your imaginary forces work," and "Think when we talk of horses that you see them."

In one scene, we show the English army attacking a French city. We pretend that the balcony at the back of the stage is the city wall. We run on stage dressed in armor, waving our swords and carrying ladders. Behind the scenes, the musicians play warlike music.

While I make my speech, the players climb up the ladders into the balcony, making as much noise as possible. Then at the end of the scene, the stagekeepers fire a cannon. It makes such a loud bang that the whole playhouse shakes.

Sword fights
Battle scenes were made realistic with sword fighting. The players were skilled sword fighters.

The Tragicall History of the Life and Death of *Doctor Faustus.*
Written by *Ch. Mar*

LONDON,
Printed for *Iohn Wright*, and are to be fold at his fhop without Newgate, at the fi.... .he
Bi¹ 1636²

17—Alleyn as Dr Faustus.

Dr. Faustus
Christopher Marlowe's *Dr. Faustus* was one of the most popular plays of the time. First performed in 1592, it was revived often over the next 50 years.

Have you ever seen a play called *Dr. Faustus?* It's about a scholar who learns how to summon up devils. He ends up being dragged off to Hell.

There's a scene in the play that always terrifies the audience. A devil suddenly appears on the stage in a cloud of smoke. Would you like to know how we do that scene? Well, take this candle and follow me down these steps. Careful now. Mind your head!

We are now under the stage. We call this space "the hell," just as we call the roof above the stage "the heavens." The devil comes down here just before he's due on stage. He waits here with two stagekeepers. Up on the stage, Dr. Faustus spouts his spells. When he has finished he raps on the floor with a long stick.

When the stagekeepers down here in the hell hear the raps, they fling open a trapdoor in the stage. The door is just above us now. Then the man playing the devil runs up a ladder and leaps through the trapdoor on to the stage while the stagekeepers set off some fireworks. It even makes me jump!

Heavens
"The heavens" was a small roof supported by two pillars. Actors playing angels, gods, or fairies were lowered from the heavens on a rope.

Dr. Faustus is taken off to Hell by a devil.

25

In some of Shakespeare's comedies, women dressed up as men as a disguise. So the boys had to play women pretending to be men.

Boy stars
The audience found the boy players totally convincing. Some boys became stars in their own right. Their roles were often as long and demanding as those of the leading men.

The boy player

My name's Nick Tooley and I'm 12 years old. Since I was 10, I've been living with Mr. Richard Burbage and his wife, Mistress Winifred. They've been better to me than my own parents.

I'm apprenticed to Mr. Burbage. That means that he is teaching me how to be a player. In return, he receives the wages I earn at the Globe. The Burbages give me good regular meals, a bed in their house, and two suits of clothes a year.

My master is a wonderful teacher. He has taught me how to walk and move on stage, and how to make myself heard all the way to the back of the playhouse. I play mostly women's roles because girls are not allowed to act. We boys have to wear big dresses, wigs, and make-up on our faces. When my voice gets deeper, I will play men.

The hardest work of all is learning all my lines. I have a part in most of the plays we put on. I often sit in the tiring house, repeating my lines over and over again until I have them all in my head.

The gallant

High fashion
Gallants' ruffs began as frilly collars and got bigger and bigger. They were replaced by standing bands in the early 1600s.

On stage
The gallants sometimes paid extra money to sit on the stage. From there, they made loud comments about the play.

Allow me to introduce myself. I'm Henry Sackville. I noticed you admiring my hat. That's an ostrich feather on top. It wasn't cheap, but you have to pay good money to keep up with the fashions here in London.

I come to the Globe every afternoon to see the other gallants and ladies, and to be seen by everyone else. I pay for my own box, which has a comfortable seat with a cushion. It's right next to the stage, where everyone can see me.

This velvet jacket, called a doublet, has pearl buttons and a silk lining. It's padded with horse hair to make my shoulders and arms look big and my waist look small. I used to wear a ruff around my neck, like most men. But this standing band is the latest thing. It's a flat collar held up by wire. Would you like me to give you the address of my tailor?

Smoking has really caught on, and I helped to start the fashion. You should have seen people's faces when I first lit a pipe at a playhouse. Someone shouted, "Look at the gallant on fire!"

The groundling

I love coming to the Globe in the afternoon, when my master gives me a penny. He's a printer, and I'm his apprentice. I stand in the yard with the other apprentices to watch a play. It costs a penny. We can't afford more than that, but we like it here. If we get bored, we throw apple cores at the players. We often make fun of the gallants with their fancy clothing up in the galleries. They look down on us and call us stinkards and groundlings, but we don't care.

My favorite player was Will Kemp. He always had something funny to say. They say that Shakespeare got angry because Kemp was always making up funnier lines than the ones written for him.

Printers
London printers had been making books since 1500. Most of them sold their books near St. Paul's Cathedral.

Stinkards
The gallants called the groundlings stinkards because their breath was said to smell of garlic.

He used to come on at the end of the play and dance a jig to a pipe and drum. Nobody can dance like Will Kemp.

Kemp has left the Globe now because he argued with the other players. It's a real shame.

Will Kemp
For a bet, Will Kemp once danced 100 miles from London to Norwich. When he got there, he jumped over a wall to show he wasn't tired.

Rough house
The Bear Garden looked a bit like a playhouse, and even had a flag flying on the top. The shows inside were rough, which appealed to the apprentices.

We apprentices work hard, but we know how to have fun too. We often play football outside the city walls. It's a rough game with no rules, and fights often break out. The Puritans would like to ban football, but we enjoy it.

There's a lot to do at Bankside. There are bowling alleys and gaming houses where people gamble with cards and dice. The Bear Garden is popular. We can see sword-fighting displays there and fights between packs of dogs, and bulls and bears.

Sometimes, an old blind bear is chained to a post while men take turns whipping him. The bear fights back and often tears the whips out of the men's hands and breaks them in half. I think it's cruel and stupid. I wish the aldermen would outlaw it.

I tell the other apprentices that they're wasting their money going to the Bear Garden. The Globe is the best place to see a show.

Easy pickings
People carried their money in purses tied with drawstrings. These were in full view, which was a great help to the cutpurses.

Thief school
Mr. Wotton, an ex-merchant, ran a real school for cutpurses. The authorities discovered it in 1585.

Begging words
Beggars in London had a secret language like the thieves. It was called Pedlar's French.

The cutpurse

There's a good crowd in the Globe today, with plenty of jingling purses to be had. I'm a cutpurse – a thief. I won't tell you my real name, but you can call me Kit. I learned my skills from the best thief in London, Mr. Wotton. He ran a school for cutpurses – until they caught him and hanged him.

I was begging on the street until Mr. Wotton took me in. There were four of us boys learning to be thieves. Mr. Wotton would hang a purse from the ceiling, with bells attached to it. We would take turns trying to lift a penny from the purse without making the bells tinkle.

Mr. Wotton taught us the language of London thieves. Picking a pocket is called "foisting." A purse is called a "bung" and a knife a "nip." So "nipping a bung" means cutting off someone's purse.

Mr. Wotton showed us the best places to steal. "Follow the crowds," he said. "Where there's a crowd, there are purses!"

Secret names
Each thief had a special name. For example, a "curber" used a long hook to steal through windows. His lookout was called a "warp."

A hanging is a good time to steal a purse. There are always crowds at one of those. I'm not fond of hangings though. They remind me of where I might end up!

I like to steal from the crowd in a playhouse, and the Globe might have been built for cutpurses! There are always lots of people there and everyone watches what's happening on stage. They are so busy looking at the play that they don't notice me with my little knife, standing right next to them with an innocent look on my face.

The best purses are to be had in the galleries, where the rich folk sit. But you have to look like a gentleman to fit in up there. Some of the older cutpurses, like the gentleman cutpurse Mr. Selman, can get away with it, but I feel much safer down in the yard.

On Sundays, the playhouses are closed. Then I pay a visit to St. Paul's Cathedral, where people go to listen to preachers talking about religion. Some of these preachers draw big crowds. But I never listen to the preachers. I'm there for the crowd and the purses.

John Selman
This man was a cutpurse who dressed as a gentleman. He was caught stealing a purse at King James's court and hanged in 1612.

Fruit gifts
Applesellers walked around the playhouses, with baskets of fruit. Gallants often offered apples to their lady friends.

The plague

Everybody knows me at the Globe. I'm Kate Strong, the appleseller. I used to come here almost every afternoon. But the playhouses have closed because a disease called the plague is spreading through London. They've just taken down the flags. The players have left town. They will be performing in the houses of lords and ladies instead. If you're wise, you won't stay here either.

In Bankside, we will all find it hard to make a living now. The watermen will have no playgoers to carry, and even the cutpurses will get hungry.

The plague seems to come with hot weather. If only a few people die the playhouses carry on. But if there are more than 30 deaths in a week, the playhouses close. Nobody knows the cause of the disease, but our government closes places where crowds gather.

Deaths
The worst summer for the plague was 1603, when more than 30,000 people died from the disease in London.

A London news sheet from the time of the plague

Closed
From 1603 to 1604, the Globe was closed for 11 months because of the plague. Some people escaped from London to the country.

Townspeople fleeing to the country to escape the plague

Rats
The real cause of the plague was the flea of the black rat. The flea carried a germ which it passed on to people as it bit them.

Treatments
Some doctors rubbed patients' heads with a dead chicken. Others gave powder that they said was made from a unicorn's horn!

There are lots of ideas about the cause of the plague. Some say it's passed on by touch, while others claim that it's caused by breathing bad air. The preachers say it has been sent by God as a punishment for our sins. Some even blame the playhouses. They say that going to plays leads people to sin. This makes God angry and so He sends the plague.

I don't know about this but I do know that the plague is a horrible disease. It killed my husband two summers ago. One day, he came home feeling hot and feverish, and he said he ached all over his body. He went to bed and he tossed and turned and sweated all night.

The next morning, I saw red swellings, as big as these apples I sell, in his armpits. I knew then that it was the plague, and Jack didn't have long to live.

We had no money for a doctor. But even if we could have afforded one, he probably wouldn't have been able to save Jack. The doctors themselves don't seem to know how to treat the plague. It kills the rich and the poor alike. May the Lord have mercy on us all.

Swellings
The plague caused certain glands to swell up. These swellings were called buboes, giving the disease its name, bubonic plague.

Henry VIII
Henry VIII was king of England from 1491 to 1547. He was the father of Queen Elizabeth I. Shakespeare's play ends with the birth of the future queen.

Fire at the Globe

On a warm sunny afternoon in June, 1613, the Globe was packed with excited and noisy playgoers. They had come to see *King Henry VIII*, a new play by Shakespeare.

Trumpets blew and the cannon was fired. All eyes were on Burbage as he strode on to the stage as the king. Nobody noticed sparks from the cannon rise through the air and land on the thatched roof.

Suddenly, a shout came from the gallery: "Fire!" The flames spread from the roof and around the playhouse. In the rush for the two narrow doors, ladies and gentlemen jostled with groundlings and players. One gallant noticed with horror that his expensive breeches were on fire. He poured a bottle of beer all over himself to douse the flames. Everyone escaped unhurt, but the Globe burned to the ground.

The next day, the preachers said the fire was a sign of God's anger at playhouses. But this did not put off the players. They immediately made plans to rebuild the Globe.

Fire risks
The Globe was unusual in having a thatched roof. Most buildings in 17th-century London had tiled roofs.

One of the last
Shakespeare co-wrote *Henry VIII* with John Fletcher, who became the Globe's main writer after Shakespeare's death in 1616.

Second globe
The Globe was rebuilt in less than a year. It had a fire-proof, tiled roof rather than a thatched one.

Closing the theaters

In 1642, a war broke out in England between King Charles I and Parliament. Parliament was the assembly that passed laws and agreed to raise new taxes for the king. From the beginning of the war, London was controlled by Parliament, whose leaders, such as Oliver Cromwell, were strict Puritans. They had always hated the theater, and in 1642 they passed a law closing the playhouses and banning the performance of all plays.

Oliver Cromwell (1599–1658)

This was a disaster for the players. Some performed illegally until they were stopped by stricter laws, fines, and whippings. Other players joined the king's army. The Globe's musicians played for the marching soldiers. The playhouses fell into disrepair and in 1644 the Globe was torn down.

King Charles lost the war and in 1649 he was beheaded. England did not have a king again until 1660, when the late king's son was crowned Charles II.

The new king loved plays, and he ordered new theaters to be built. These were very different from the Globe. They were indoor theaters where actors, including women, performed for small wealthy audiences. There was a new kind of stage too, with painted backdrops making each scene look like a picture of real life.

Banning fun
The Puritans banned all kinds of fun – dancing on May Day, football, and even Christmas.

Love interest
The most famous actress of the 1660s was Nell Gwynn. King Charles II fell in love with her. She bore him two sons.

Shakespeare today

Although the Globe was torn down, Shakespeare's works lived on. When the new theaters opened in the 1660s, some of the first plays to be performed were by Shakespeare.

His plays became so popular that they changed the English language. Every day, English speakers use phrases invented by the famous playwright.

Shakespeare's plays have been translated into many languages. They are performed in theaters, and shown in movie houses all over the world.

In 1997, a replica of the Globe opened near the site of the original. Here you can watch a play from the yard like a groundling, or from the galleries like a gallant – just as people did in Shakespeare's time.

Henry V being performed at the Globe theater in 1997

Hit film
One of the most popular films of 1996 was William Shakespeare's *Romeo and Juliet*, starring Leonardo di Caprio and Claire Danes. The film was set in modern times but used most of the original text.

Men as women
The modern Globe has experimented with boys and men playing female roles. In 1999, the actor Mark Rylance played Cleopatra.

Glossary

Alderman
Member of the council, or body of men that ruled a city, such as London.

Apprentices
Teenage boys and young men learning a trade.

Bear garden
Building where bears fought dogs, bulls, or men armed with whips, for entertainment.

Bubo
Swelling caused by the plague, found in the armpit or groin.

Backdrop
Painted cloth hung on the wall behind the stage, to set the scene.

Comedy
A light-hearted play with a happy ending.

Cutpurse
A thief who stole purses and picked pockets.

Gallant
A young man who was a leader of fashion.

Groundling
Someone who paid to stand in the yard of a theater to see a play.

Heavens
The roofed area above the stage in a theater.

Hell
The space beneath the stage in a theater.

Jig
A dance to a pipe and drum, often performed at the end of a play.

Lease
An agreement, allowing someone to use a building or piece of land for a set period.

Lord Chamberlain
Title of an important nobleman who helped the king or queen to rule the country.

Plague
A deadly disease. There were several types of plague. In the 1600s, the worst outbreaks were of bubonic plague.

Preacher
Someone who makes speeches about religion, to teach the public.

Puritans
Strict Christians who believed that it was wrong to seek worldly pleasures such as music, dancing, and playgoing.

Playhouse
Sixteenth-century name for a theater – a house where plays are performed.

Ruff
Frill around the neck made from starched linen or cotton.

Stage
The wooden platform where the actors stood to perform their plays.

Stagekeeper
Hired men who did odd jobs in the playhouse, such as moving scenery and firing the cannon.

Stinkard
Nickname given to poor people, who were supposed to smell bad because they ate raw garlic and seldom washed.

Tiring house
Dressing room behind the stage where costumes and props were stored. "Tiring" means dressing.

Tragedy
A serious play with a sad ending.

Traveling player
An actor whose company moved from place to place, putting on plays in market-places and inn-yards.

Waterman
A man who made a living by rowing boats on a river, carrying passengers or goods.